D1152855

Mustard, Custard, Grumble Belly and Gravy

This edition published in Great Britain in 2006 by
Bloomsbury Publishing Plc
36 Soho Square, London, W1D 3QY
Text copyright © Michael Rosen, 2006
Illustrations copyright © Quentin Blake, 2006

Don't Put Mustard in the Custard first published in hardback by André Deutsch Ltd, 1985
Text copyright © Michael Rosen, 1985
Illustrations copyright © Quentin Blake, 1985

You Can't Catch Me first published in hardback by André Deutsch Ltd, 1981
Text copyright © Michael Rosen, 1981
Illustrations copyright © Quentin Blake, 1981

The moral right of the author and illustrator has been asserted

A CIP catalogue record of this book is available from the British Library

ISBN 0 7475 8739 6
ISBN-13 9780747587392

All papers used by Bloomsbury Publishing are natural, recyclable products
made from wood grown in well-managed forests. The manufacturing processes
conform to the environmental regulations of the country of origin.

Printed in China

1 3 5 7 9 10 8 6 4 2

www.bloomsbury.com

Mustard, Custard, Grumble Belly and Gravy

Michael Rosen · Quentin Blake

BLOOMSBURY
CHILDREN'S
BOOKS

Mustard, Custard, Grumble Belly and Gravy

Twenty-five years ago, Quentin Blake and I came together to create one of the first all-colour poetry books of new poems for children, **You Can't Catch Me** and then we followed this up a few years later with **Don't Put Mustard in the Custard**. It's these two books which Bloomsbury have combined in this one volume.

We often think of reading as a silent, solitary activity, and, yes, it often is. But it can also be a shared, out-loud, public moment – some halfway house between private reading and having a chat with friends. For children, this means it can be a vital link between their talk and the ability to read books to themselves straight off the page. My poems are mostly made up out of the words and phrases and sounds I've caught off the air, whizzing past me as uttered by my brother, my parents, my friends and my children. This means that they sit on the page longing for you to say them out loud, to set them whizzing all over again. And the great thing about poems is that you don't have to be the person who wrote them to perform them. You can say them in whatever voice you fancy.

When I read these poems out loud, I do that and more: I act them out, almost as if I'm living out Quentin's drawings! If you get any pleasure out of putting on voices or becoming another person, then what I've written here will give you the material for a whole number of bed-time, car-journey or classroom performances.

Like most poets, I have a go at writing about a variety of things and in a variety of ways. This means that what you find here are snatches of conversation,

alongside fantasies, nonsense, word-play, argument, moments of sadness and euphoric mucking about. Sometimes the sound of the words, the rhyme, the rhythm and repetition come through loud and clear. The reason why we seem to love this kind of musical poetry might seem mysterious. My own view is that it comes from how everyday language sounds in our minds when we are young. That's to say, much of it sounds very clear but means next to nothing. It's as if our ears can tune in to it, but for quite a lot of the time, our minds can't. A lot of the language that we hear when we are children, then, is sound-only, or sound-mainly. And when we see word-play that we can recognise as word-play, it all starts getting very ticklish and exciting. In a way, it gives us a sense of satisfaction that we 'get it'. It's these ticklish hooks which will also carry us on into phrases and ideas that for the present we may not totally grasp but soon will.

I sometimes write pieces that seem much less musical, almost like fragments of chat or thought. When I work with children, I call this 'talking on to the page with my pen'. I do this because I believe the page is a good place to put these moments, memories, scenes, dreams and fragments. The way we talk is a fine way of communicating, so why not talk on to a page? It suits me down to the ground to be doing this, and I've always felt that it might also suit plenty of you too. Many of you will find talking much easier to do than writing, so why not bridge the gap and see if you can talk on to the page? I hope that these poems will help you do just that!

And then there's this thing we call Nonsense. There's a lot of nonsense written about Nonsense, so I'll try to avoid doing the same. I think we sometimes like words and language to be odd, absurd, surreal or meaningless because, when we read it, for that moment we're released from all that struggle and brain-work of turning what we hear into what we think it's supposed to mean. As we say, it's silly, weird, upside-down and crazy – all words that suggest that Nonsense belongs in some kind of parallel world where the usual rules don't work. After a hard hour's thinking, that can be quite a nice place to live in for a while.

Finally, I'm often asked how Quentin and I make a book and I'm always happy to say that it mostly involves me handing over some pages of writing and leaving the rest to him. Really! The whole thing. This means that he not only draws and paints without me looking over his shoulder but he also plans and designs the book. This way what you see is a truly joint venture: it's my work re-invented by Quentin. I'm lucky to be able to look back at these poems and pictures as if they've had 25 years of life with children, parents, uncles, aunts, grandparents and teachers and, in fact, the 'Don't Put Mustard in the Custard' poem was voted as the best loved poem for children by a living poet. I hope you enjoy this new edition of the poems just as much.

Michael Rosen

DON'T

PUT MUSTARD

IN THE CUSTARD

STAMP STAMP STAMP

You can hide in our house

you can make a camp

you can march all round our house

stamp stamp stamp.

TRAINERS

See me in my trainers
speeding round the house
see me in my trainers
speeding down the street
see me in my trainers
speeding to the shops.

See me in my trainers
kicking a tennis ball

see me in my trainers
kicking a hard brick wall

see me in my trainers
kicking my friend's leg.

See me in my trainers
there's a hole in my toe
see me in my trainers
the sole's worn through

you can't see me in my trainers

they're in the dustbin.

See my trainers.

DON'T

Don't do,
Don't do,
Don't do that.
Don't pull faces,
Don't tease the cat.

Don't pick your ears,
Don't be rude at school.
Who do they think I am?

Some kind of fool?

One day
they'll say
Don't put toffee in my coffee
don't pour gravy on the baby
don't put beer in his ear
don't stick your toes up his nose.

Don't put confetti on the spaghetti
and don't squash peas on your knees.

Don't put ants in your pants
don't put mustard in the custard

don't chuck jelly at the telly

and don't throw fruit at a computer

don't throw fruit at a computer.

Don't what?

Don't throw fruit at a computer.

Don't what?

Don't throw fruit at a computer.

Who do they think I am?

Some kind of fool?

WATER

Water is what you put with
everything else
to make it not taste like water.
Sometimes you can't see it
and you have to put your hands in it
to find out if it's there.
Then people say you get soft water
and hard water.
It all feels soft to me.
Sometimes cold. Sometimes hot.

Sometimes very cold – and it goes into ice.

That's hard.

Sometimes very hot and you get steam in the bathroom.

I like it best of all

with salt

in the sea.

Though snow is good too.

DIGITAL WATCH

Digital Fidgetal Botch
a fly got into my watch.

The digit digitted
the fly fidgeted.
Digital Fidgetal Botch.

Tiffy Taffy

Tiffy taffy toffee
on the flee flo floor.
Tiffy taffy toffee
on the dee doe door.
Kiffy kaffy coffee
in a jig jag jug.
Kiffy kaffy coffee
in a mig mag mug.

VIDEO

Oh video oh video
the video the diddy-o
twiddly-o the video
the video the diddle.

SOMETHING'S DRASTIC

Something's drastic
my nose is made of plastic
something's drastic
my ears are elastic
something's drastic
something's drastic.
I'm fantastic!

I'M CARRYING THE BABY

Eddie was three.
"Look at me," he said,
"look at me
I'm carrying the baby
look at me
look at me
I'm carrying the baby."

"Oh," said Eddie,
"look at me
I've dropped the baby."

NURSERY

My mum says
once I came home from nursery
with a sulky look on my face.

"What's the matter?" she said.
I said nothing.
"What's the matter?" she said.
I said nothing.
 "What's the matter?"
"I had to sit on the naughty chair."

"Why did you have to sit on the naughty chair?"
I said nothing.
"Why did you have to sit on the naughty chair?"
"Cos I was being naughty."
"Yes yes, I guessed that," she says,
"But what were you doing?"

"I was playing about at singing time,

"I wasn't singing the right things."

"What was everyone singing?"

"Baa baa black sheep."

"And what were you singing?"

"Baa-baa moo-moo."

BATHROOM FIDDLER

I'm the bathroom fiddler
the bathroom twiddler
the foodler and the doodler
the dawdler and the diddler.
I dibble and I dabble
I meddle and I muddle
when it's time for me to wash
when I know it's time for bed.

When I go up to the bathroom
to get ready for bed
I don't get washed straightaway
I fiddle and I diddle.

I pick up the toothbrush
and I bite the bristles,
I get the bristles in my teeth and I pull
I pull
I heave
I have a tug-of-war with the toothbrush
I'm winning I'm winning
yeurchk – my mouth's full of bristles.

I get the can of talcum powder
I hold it in my hand
I drop my hand down fast
and out comes a puff of powder
catch the cloud of powder
but it falls to the floor
hey, it's snowing in here.

I make mixtures in the sink
pour in the shampoo and the bubble bath
whisk it all up to make the bubbles

then I say,
"OK you Bubbles, you're finished."
At that,
I blow huge puffs of air
and the bubbles pop all over the place.

Then I stick my finger down the plughole

and scoop out the mucky stuff down there

and then I stand and dream

sucking on the sponge

and then I stand and dream

sucking on the sponge

and dream sucking on the sponge

sucking on the sponge

on the sponge

the sponge

sponge.

DON'T TELL

Christmas eve
Christmas day
don't tell mum I'm running away.

I'm afraid of Father Christmas
coming down the chimney
while I'm fast asleep
he might come and grab me.

Christmas eve
Christmas day
don't tell mum
I'm running away.

GONE

She sat in the back of the van
and we waved to her there

we ran towards her
but the van moved off

we ran faster
she reached out for us

the van moved faster
we reached for her hand

she stretched out of the back of the van
we ran, reaching

the van got away
we stopped running

we never reached her
before she was gone.

THE GREATEST

I'm the world's greatest at sport

I've won gold medals for

underwater tennis

nose throwing

elbow climbing

potato jumping

snail lifting

and computer wrestling.

I'm the world's greatest inventor

I've invented

a dog scrambler

a sock mixer

a throat cleaner

a moustache toaster

and a custard sprinkler.

I'm the world's greatest.

WHO LIKES CUDDLES

Who likes cuddles?

Me.

Who likes hugs?

Me.

Who likes squeezes?

Me.

Who likes tickles?

Me.

Who likes getting their face stroked?

Me.

Who likes being lifted up high?

Me.

Who likes sitting on laps?

Me.

Who likes being whirled round and round?

Me.

But best of all I like
getting into bed and getting blowy blowy
down my neck behind my ear.
A big warm tickly blow
lovely.

KEITH'S CUPBOARD

Have you ever looked in Keith's cupboard?
You ought to.
You've never seen anything like Keith's cupboard.
Let's go over to Keith's place
and look in Keith's cupboard.

So when you get to Keith's place
you say,
"Can we play with your garage?"
And he says,
"No."
So you say,
"Can we play in your tent?"
And he says,
"No."
So you say,
"Can we play with your crane?"
And he says,
"No."

So you go up to Keith's mum
and you say,
"Can we play in Keith's tent?"
And she says,
"Keith, Keith,
why don't you get the tent out?"
"OK,"
says Keith,
and he starts going over to the cupboard –
Keith's cupboard.
He opens it, and –
Phew!

You've never seen anything like
Keith's cupboard.
In it
there's trucks, and garages, and tents
and cranes and forts and bikes and puppets
and games, and models and superhero suits
and hats and
he never plays with any of it.

They keep buying him all this stuff
and he never plays with it.

Day after day after day
it all sits in Keith's cupboard.

You ought to go over to his place sometime
and have a look.
Keith's cupboard.
Phew!

NIGHTMARE

I'm down
I'm underground

I'm down the Undeground

Waiting

Waiting for a train

There's the platform
There's the lines
There's the tunnel
There's the lines.

I'll wait down there
Down between the lines
Waiting for the train
Down between the lines.
I'll climb down there
Down between the lines
and wait for the train
down there.

Look

Look up the tunnel look
Yes it's coming, it's coming
they say,

And it is.
And I'm between the lines.

And I can see it
See it coming
and I'm between the lines.

Can someone give me a
hand up?
Can't you see?

I'm between the lines
and the train's coming.
Can't you see?

I'm between the lines
and the train's coming.
Give me a hand someone
give me a hand
the train's coming
give me a hand
I can't climb up.
The train's coming

and the platform's sliding in
towards me too
with the train still coming
coming down the tunnel
the platform's sliding
sliding in towards me too.

I'm still down
Can't anyone see me
down between the lines?

Look

see

me

the train

platform

me

the train

near now

nearer now

nearer and nearer now

NOW

That's all.

BELLYACHE

I've got a belly-ache

It's right in the middle of my belly.

It's like a great big grumbling doughnut
It's like a hedgehog in there.

I've got a belly-ache
I've put a hot water bottle on it.
Didn't make it better.
I've taken really deep breaths
Didn't make it better.
I've rubbed it all over
Didn't make it better.

I want that great big grumbling doughnut to float away
I want that hedgehog to shrink.

I've got a bellyache
and it won't go away

WHO? WHY? WHERE? WHAT?

Who invented spoons?

I don't know.

Do buffaloes eat spaghetti?

I don't know.

Why do people go to sleep?

Because – er because – er

What was the first egg in the world?

I don't know.

Where was I before I was born?

You were – er you weren't – er –

If I could turn my head round and round

could I walk backwards looking forwards?

Could you stop asking me questions?

I'm Big

I'm big

I'm very big

Because I'm very big

I can grab your pen

and you're scared

to try and get your pen back

because I'm big.

Very big.

But I've heard that
when people grow up
some people grow faster
than others.

This means that
when I'm grown up
you may be big
and I may be
not so big.

This is one of the things I worry about.

STUNTMAN

I say:

I'm a stuntman

I'm a stuntman

I can jump off two stairs.

He says:

Yes – jump off two stairs.

Then I jump off.

I say:

I can jump off four stairs.

He says:

Yes – jump off four stairs.

Then I jump.

I say:

I can jump off eight stairs.

He says:

Yes, jump off eight stairs.

Then I jump.

I shout:

Look at me I'm a stuntman.

He says:

Yes, you are a stuntman.

Then I say:

Now you can be a stuntman if you like

What do you want to do?

And he says:

You lie down on the floor

And I'll jump on you.

LAST WORD

Dad says:

Stop doing that:

So the boy stuck his tongue out.

Dad says:

Don't stick your tongue out at me.

So the boy says:

I'm not. I'm just licking my lips.

Later:

BANG BANG BANG BANG.

Dad says:

Stop jumping up and down there

I can't stand the noise.

And the girl says:

I'm not jumping. I'm hopping.

Dad says:

Some people always get the last word.

SAY PLEASE

I'll have a please sandwich cheese

No I mean a knees sandwich please

Sorry I mean a fleas sandwich please

No a please sandwich please
No   No –

I'll have a doughnut.

YOU CAN'T CATCH ME!

STOP!

Every few weeks someone looks at me and says:

my you've grown

and then every few weeks someone says:

they've grown too long

and silver scissors come out of the drawer

and chip at my toes and run through my hair.

Now I don't like this one little bit.

I won't grow if I'm going to be chopped.

What's me is mine and I want to keep it

so either me or the scissors or my nails had better stop.

THE YOUNGEST

I'm the youngest in our house
So it goes like this:

My brother comes in and says:
"Tell him to clear the fluff
out from under his bed."
Mum says,
"Clear the fluff
out from under your bed."
Father says,
"You heard what your mother said."
"What?" I say.
"The fluff," he says.
"Clear the fluff
out from under your bed."
So I say,
"There's fluff under his bed, too,
you know."

So father says,
"But we're talking about the fluff
under *your* bed."
"You will clear it up
won't you?" mum says.
So now my brother – all puffed up –
says,
"Clear the fluff
out from under your bed,
clear the fluff
out from under your bed."
Now I'm angry. I am angry.
So I say – what shall I say?
I say,
"Shuttup, Stinks!
YOU CAN'T RULE MY LIFE."

RANZO

Who rolled in the mud
behind the garage door?
Who left footprints
across the kitchen floor?

I know a dog whose nose is cold
I know a dog whose nose is cold

Who chased raindrops
down the windows?
Who smudged the glass
with the end of his nose?

I know a dog with a cold in his nose
I know a dog with a cold in his nose

Who wants a bath
and a big crunchy biscuit?
Who wants to bed down
in his fireside basket?

Me, said Ranzo
I'm the dog with a cold.

SHORTS

Long shorts
short longs
short shorts
long shorts up high
long shorts down low
long longs on his head.

JOHNNY

Johnny ran away

to join the merchant navy

but he came back the very next day

and drank up all the gravy.

SHOES

If you don't put your shoes on before I count fifteen

then we won't go to the woods to climb the chestnut tree.

One.

But I can't find them.

Two.

I can't.

They're under the sofa. Three.

No … O yes.

Four Five Six.

Stop – they've got knots they've got knots.

You should untie the laces when you take your shoes

off. Seven.

Will you do one shoe while I do the other
then?
Eight. But that would be cheating …
Please.
All right.
It always …
Nine.
It always sticks – I'll use my teeth.
Ten.
It won't it won't … It has – look.

Eleven.

I'm not wearing any socks.

Twelve.

Stop counting stop counting. (Mum where

are my socks mum?)

THEY'RE IN YOUR SHOES. WHERE YOU LEFT THEM.

I didn't.

Thirteen.

O they're inside out and upside down and

bundled up.

Fourteen.

Have you done the knot on the shoe you

were …

Yes. Put it on the right foot.

But socks don't have right and wrong foot.

The shoes, silly … Fourteen and a half.

I am I am. Wait.

Don't go to the woods without me.

Look that's one shoe already.

Fourteen and threequarters.

There!

You haven't tied the bows yet.

We could do them on the way there?

No we won't. Fourteen and seven eighths.

Help me then –

You know I'm not fast at bows.

Fourteen and fifteen sixteeeenths.

A single bow is all right, isn't it?

Fifteen. We're off.

See I did it.

Didn't I?

WAITER AND JUSTER

My mum had nicknames for me and my brother.
One of us she called Waiter
and the other she called Juster.
It started like this:
She'd say, "Lend me a hand with the washing up
will you, you two?"
And I'd say, "Just a minute, Mum,"
and my brother'd say,
"Wait a minute, Mum."
"There you go again" – she'd say,
"Juster and Waiter."

Mm?

I say:

What are you doing? And our little boy Joe says,

Mm?

What d'you think you're doing?

Mm?

Why did you do that?

Mm?

The peanut butter. All over your blanket.

Mm?

And the talcum powder?

Mm?

Don't do it – do you understand?

Mm?

Or there'll be trouble. And Joe says,

Trouble,

and runs off laughing.

The Longest Journey in the World

"Last one into bed
has to switch out the light."
It's just the same every night.
There's a race.
I'm ripping off my trousers and shirt –
he's kicking off his shoes and socks.

"My sleeve's stuck."
"This button's too big for its button-hole."
"Have you hidden my pyjamas?"
"Keep your hands off mine."
If you win
you get where it's safe
before the darkness comes –
but if you lose
if you're last
you know what you've got coming up is
the journey from the light switch
to your bed.
It's the Longest Journey in the World.

"You're last tonight," my brother says.
And he's right.
There is nowhere so dark
as that room in the moment
after I've switched out the light.

There is nowhere so full of dangerous things –
things that love dark places –
things that breathe only when you breathe
and hold their breath when I hold mine.
So I have to say:
"I'm not scared."

That face, grinning in the pattern on the wall

isn't a face —

"I'm not scared."

That prickle on the back of my neck

is only the label on my pyjama jacket —

"I'm not scared."

That moaning-moaning is nothing

but water in a pipe —

"I'm not scared."

Everything's going to be just fine

as soon as I get into that bed of mine.

Such a terrible shame

it's always the same

it takes so long

it takes so long

it takes so long

to get there.

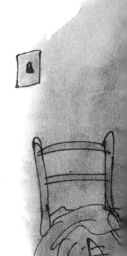

From the light switch
to my bed.
It's the Longest Journey in the World.

NOSE

You say: let me have your nose
I would like to use it today.

And I say: but it's the only one I've got
you can't take my nose away.

DANNY

Your brother Danny's got a golden nose
and fish swim out of his eyes.
Your brother Danny's got legs like rhubarb
and ears like apple pies.

GRUMBLE BELLY

"You can't catch me, GRUMBLE BELLY."

"Don't want to."

"You couldn't if you wanted to, GRUMBLE BELLY."

"I wouldn't if I could."

"You're too slow, GRUMBLE PUMP."

"Oh am I?"

"You can't catch me, GRUMBLE PUMP PUMP."

"I'm very, very, very slow but when I'm quick

I'LL GET YOU ...

I've got you
I've got you
and I'll never let you go."

Purple

I saw a lady with red hair
talking to one with blue on.

The sun shone
and the rain ran
the streets emptied
the people had gone …

When I looked
for the ladies again
there was a purple stream
flowing down the drain.

JIM

Down behind the dustbin
I met a dog called Jim.
He didn't know me
and I didn't know him.

SID

Down behind the dustbin
I met a dog called Sid.
He could smell a bone inside
but couldn't lift the lid.

Jojo

I am Jojo
give me the sun to eat.
I am Jojo
give me the moon to suck.

The waters of my mouth
will put out the fires of the sun;
the waters of my mouth
will melt the light of the moon.

Day becomes night,
night becomes day.
I am Jojo
listen to what I say.

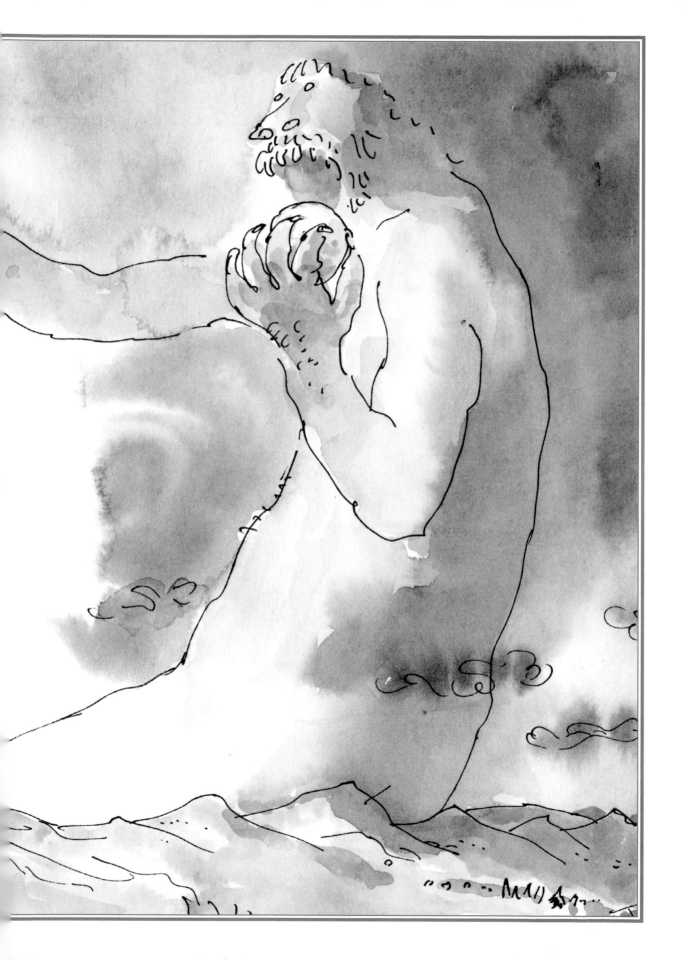

Tip-top tip-top

tap a speckled egg.

Once to put him in his cup

and twice to crack his head.

PEAS

Peas for breakfast please he said
and a plateful of peas is what he got

and when he went to bed last night
I heard him say: more peas please.

You know, I don't think he eats much else
one full bowl three times a day.

It would fill a room all those peas you know
but I think
even if he had to wade up to his knees in peas
he would still come here saying: more peas please.

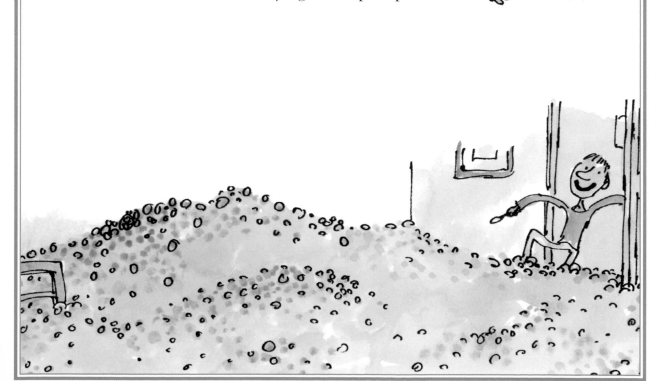

BOAT

Made a boat
from sticks and cloth –
put it on the water
to see it float.

Go boat, go boat
sail across that sea.
Go boat
and sail on back to me.

It's sea and sky all the way over
my boat flies out across the water
but always comes on back to me.

It's a good boat
go boat.
She's a sail boat
my boat.

Go boat, go boat
sail across that sea.
Go boat
and sail on back to me.

THIS IS THE HAND

This is the hand
that touched the frost
that froze my tongue
and made it numb.

This is the hand
that cracked the nut
that went in my mouth
and never came out.

This is the hand
that slid round the bath
to find the soap
that wouldn't float.

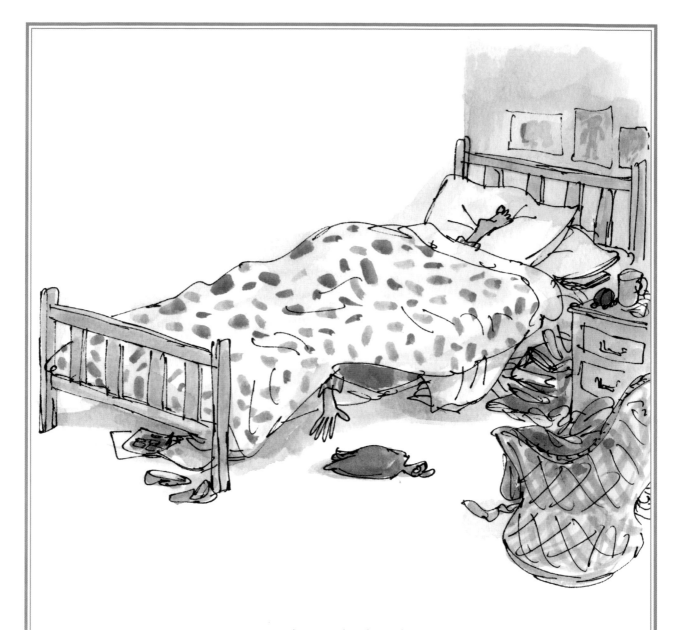

This is the hand
on the hot water bottle
meant to warm my bed
that got lost instead.

This is the hand
that held the bottle
that let go of the soap
that cracked the nut
that touched the frost.
This is the hand
that never gets lost.

To Sea

I put out to sea
in a wooden row-boat
with a cheese and pickle sandwich
and a yellow hat and coat.

HE DID

Down behind the dustbin
I met a dog called Sid.
He said he didn't know me,
but I'm pretty sure he did.